If Lost, Please Return This Planner To:

_____

2020 At A Glance

January

S	M	T	W	T	F	S
			1	2	3	4
5	6	7	8	9	10	11
12	13	14	15	16	17	18
19	20	21	22	23	24	25
26	27	28	29	30	31	

February

S	M	T	W	T	F	S
						1
2	3	4	5	6	7	8
9	10	11	12	13	14	15
16	17	18	19	20	21	22
23	24	25	26	27	28	29

March

S	M	T	W	T	F	S
1	2	3	4	5	6	7
8	9	10	11	12	13	14
15	16	17	18	19	20	21
22	23	24	25	26	27	28
29	30	31				

April

S	M	T	W	T	F	S
			1	2	3	4
5	6	7	8	9	10	11
12	13	14	15	16	17	18
19	20	21	22	23	24	25
26	27	28	29	30		

May

S	M	T	W	T	F	S
					1	2
3	4	5	6	7	8	9
10	11	12	13	14	15	16
17	18	19	20	21	22	23
24	25	26	27	28	29	30
31						

June

S	M	T	W	T	F	S
	1	2	3	4	5	6
7	8	9	10	11	12	13
14	15	16	17	18	19	20
21	22	23	24	25	26	27
28	29	30				

July

S	M	T	W	T	F	S
			1	2	3	4
5	6	7	8	9	10	11
12	13	14	15	16	17	18
19	20	21	22	23	24	25
26	27	28	29	30	31	

August

S	M	T	W	T	F	S
						1
2	3	4	5	6	7	8
9	10	11	12	13	14	15
16	17	18	19	20	21	22
23	24	25	26	27	28	29
30	31					

September

S	M	T	W	T	F	S
		1	2	3	4	5
6	7	8	9	10	11	12
13	14	15	16	17	18	19
20	21	22	23	24	25	26
27	28	29	30			

October

S	M	T	W	T	F	S
				1	2	3
4	5	6	7	8	9	10
11	12	13	14	15	16	17
18	19	20	21	22	23	24
25	26	27	28	29	30	31

November

S	M	T	W	T	F	S
1	2	3	4	5	6	7
8	9	10	11	12	13	14
15	16	17	18	19	20	21
22	23	24	25	26	27	28
29	30					

December

S	M	T	W	T	F	S
		1	2	3	4	5
6	7	8	9	10	11	12
13	14	15	16	17	18	19
20	21	22	23	24	25	26
27	28	29	30	31		

January 1-4

This Week

_____

_____

_____

_____

_____

_____

_____

_____

_____

_____

_____

_____

_____

_____

_____

_____

_____

_____

_____

1 Wednesday

2 Thursday

3 Friday

4 Saturday

January 5-11

This Week

_____
_____
_____
_____
_____
_____
_____
_____
_____
_____
_____
_____
_____
_____
_____
_____
_____
_____
_____
_____

5 Sunday

6 Monday

7 Tuesday

8 Wednesday

9 Thursday

10 Friday

11 Saturday

Notes

top priorities for this week

_____
_____
_____
_____
_____

Victories for the week

looking ahead to next week

_____
_____
_____
_____
_____
_____
_____
_____

January 12-18

This Week

_____

_____

_____

_____

_____

_____

_____

_____

_____

_____

_____

_____

_____

_____

_____

_____

_____

_____

_____

_____

_____

_____

12 Sunday
13 Monday
14 Tuesday
15 Wednesday

16 Thursday

17 Friday

18 Saturday

Notes

top priorities for this week

_____

_____

_____

_____

_____

Victories for the week

looking ahead to next week

_____

_____

_____

_____

_____

_____

_____

January 19-25

This Week

_____
_____
_____
_____
_____
_____
_____
_____
_____
_____
_____
_____
_____
_____
_____
_____
_____
_____
_____
_____
_____

19 Sunday

20 Monday

21 Tuesday

22 Wednesday

23 Thursday

24 Friday

25 Saturday

Notes

top priorities for this week

_____
_____
_____
_____
_____
_____

Victories for the week

looking ahead to next week

_____
_____
_____
_____
_____
_____
_____
_____
_____

January 26-February 1

This Week

_____
_____
_____
_____
_____
_____
_____
_____
_____
_____
_____
_____
_____
_____
_____
_____
_____
_____
_____

26 Sunday
27 Monday
28 Tuesday
29 Wednesday

30 Thursday	top priorities for this week
	_____
	_____
	_____
	_____
31 Friday	
	┌─────────────────────┐
	│ Victories for the week │
	│ │
	│ │
	│ │
1 Saturday	│ │
	└─────────────────────┘
	looking ahead to next week
Notes	_____
	_____
	_____
	_____
	_____
	_____
	_____

February 2-8

This Week

_____

_____

_____

_____

_____

_____

_____

_____

_____

_____

_____

_____

_____

_____

_____

_____

_____

_____

_____

2 Sunday
3 Monday
4 Tuesday
5 Wednesday

6 Thursday

7 Friday

8 Saturday

Notes

top priorities for this week

_____
_____
_____
_____
_____

Victories for the week

looking ahead to next week

_____
_____
_____
_____
_____
_____
_____
_____

February 9-15

This Week

_____
_____
_____
_____
_____
_____
_____
_____
_____
_____
_____
_____
_____
_____
_____
_____
_____
_____
_____
_____
_____

9 Sunday

10 Monday

11 Tuesday

12 Wednesday

13 Thursday

14 Friday

15 Saturday

Notes

top priorities for this week

_____
_____
_____
_____

Victories for the week

looking ahead to next week

_____
_____
_____
_____
_____
_____
_____

February 16-22

This Week

_____

_____

_____

_____

_____

_____

_____

_____

_____

_____

_____

_____

_____

_____

_____

_____

_____

_____

_____

_____

_____

16 Sunday

17 Monday

18 Tuesday

19 Wednesday

20 Thursday

21 Friday

22 Saturday

Notes

top priorities for this week

_____
_____
_____
_____
_____
_____

Victories for the week

looking ahead to next week

_____
_____
_____
_____
_____
_____
_____
_____

February 23-29

This Week

_____

_____

_____

_____

_____

_____

_____

_____

_____

_____

_____

_____

_____

_____

_____

_____

_____

_____

_____

_____

_____

_____

23 Sunday

24 Monday

25 Tuesday

26 Wednesday

27 Thursday

28 Friday

29 Saturday

Notes

top priorities for this week

_____
_____
_____
_____
_____

Victories for the week

looking ahead to next week

_____
_____
_____
_____
_____
_____
_____
_____

March 1-7

This Week

_____
_____
_____
_____
_____
_____
_____
_____
_____
_____
_____
_____
_____
_____
_____
_____
_____
_____
_____
_____

1 Sunday
2 Monday
3 Tuesday
4 Wednesday

5   Thursday

6   Friday

7   Saturday

Notes

top priorities for this week

_____
_____
_____
_____
_____
_____

Victories for the week

looking ahead to next week

_____
_____
_____
_____
_____
_____
_____
_____

March 8-14

This Week

_____
_____
_____
_____
_____
_____
_____
_____
_____
_____
_____
_____
_____
_____
_____
_____
_____
_____
_____
_____
_____
_____
_____

8 Sunday
9 Monday
10 Tuesday
11 Wednesday

12 Thursday

13 Friday

14 Saturday

Notes

top priorities for this week

_____
_____
_____
_____
_____

Victories for the week

looking ahead to next week

_____
_____
_____
_____
_____
_____
_____
_____

March 15-21

This Week

_____
_____
_____
_____
_____
_____
_____
_____
_____
_____
_____
_____
_____
_____
_____
_____
_____
_____
_____

15 Sunday

16 Monday

17 Tuesday

18 Wednesday

19 Thursday

20 Friday

21 Saturday

Notes

top priorities for this week

_____
_____
_____
_____
_____
_____

Victories for the week

looking ahead to next week

_____
_____
_____
_____
_____
_____
_____
_____
_____

March 22-28

This Week

_____
_____
_____
_____
_____
_____
_____
_____
_____
_____
_____
_____
_____
_____
_____
_____
_____
_____
_____
_____
_____

22 Sunday

23 Monday

24 Tuesday

25 Wednesday

26 Thursday

27 Friday

28 Saturday

Notes

top priorities for this week

_____
_____
_____
_____
_____
_____

Victories for the week

looking ahead to next week

_____
_____
_____
_____
_____
_____
_____
_____
_____

March 29-April 4

This Week

_____
_____
_____
_____
_____
_____
_____
_____
_____
_____
_____
_____
_____
_____
_____
_____
_____
_____
_____
_____
_____

29 Sunday

30 Monday

31 Tuesday

1 Wednesday

2 Thursday

3 Friday

4 Saturday

Notes

top priorities for this week

_____
_____
_____
_____
_____

Victories for the week

looking ahead to next week

_____
_____
_____
_____
_____
_____
_____

April 5-11

This Week

_____
_____
_____
_____
_____
_____
_____
_____
_____
_____
_____
_____
_____
_____
_____
_____
_____
_____
_____

5 Sunday

6 Monday

7 Tuesday

8 Wednesday

9   Thursday

10   Friday

11   Saturday

Notes

top priorities for this week
_____
_____
_____
_____
_____

Victories for the week

looking ahead to next week
_____
_____
_____
_____
_____
_____
_____

April 12-18

This Week

_____
_____
_____
_____
_____
_____
_____
_____
_____
_____
_____
_____
_____
_____
_____
_____
_____
_____
_____

12 Sunday

13 Monday

14 Tuesday

15 Wednesday

16 Thursday

17 Friday

18 Saturday

Notes

top priorities for this week

_____
_____
_____
_____
_____

Victories for the week

looking ahead to next week

_____
_____
_____
_____
_____
_____
_____

April 19-25

This Week

_____

_____

_____

_____

_____

_____

_____

_____

_____

_____

_____

_____

_____

_____

_____

_____

_____

_____

_____

19 Sunday
20 Monday
21 Tuesday
22 Wednesday

23 Thursday

24 Friday

25 Saturday

Notes

top priorities for this week

_____
_____
_____
_____
_____

Victories for the week

looking ahead to next week

_____
_____
_____
_____
_____
_____
_____
_____

April 26-May 2

This Week

_____

_____

_____

_____

_____

_____

_____

_____

_____

_____

_____

_____

_____

_____

_____

_____

_____

_____

26 Sunday

27 Monday

28 Tuesday

29 Wednesday

30 Thursday

1 Friday

2 Saturday

Notes

top priorities for this week

_____
_____
_____
_____
_____
_____

Victories for the week

looking ahead to next week

_____
_____
_____
_____
_____
_____
_____

May 3-9

This Week

_____
_____
_____
_____
_____
_____
_____
_____
_____
_____
_____
_____
_____
_____
_____
_____
_____
_____
_____
_____
_____

3 Sunday

4 Monday

5 Tuesday

6 Wednesday

7 Thursday

8 Friday

9 Saturday

Notes

top priorities for this week

_____
_____
_____
_____
_____

Victories for the week

looking ahead to next week

_____
_____
_____
_____
_____
_____
_____
_____

May 10-16

This Week

_____
_____
_____
_____
_____
_____
_____
_____
_____
_____
_____
_____
_____
_____
_____
_____
_____
_____

10 Sunday
11 Monday
12 Tuesday
13 Wednesday

14 Thursday

15 Friday

16 Saturday

Notes

top priorities for this week

_____
_____
_____
_____
_____

Victories for the week

looking ahead to next week

_____
_____
_____
_____
_____
_____
_____

May 17-23

This Week

_____
_____
_____
_____
_____
_____
_____
_____
_____
_____
_____
_____
_____
_____
_____
_____
_____
_____
_____
_____

17	Sunday
18	Monday
17	Sunday
20	Wednesday

21 Thursday

22 Friday

23 Saturday

Notes

Victories for the week

looking ahead to next week

May 24-30

This Week

_____
_____
_____
_____

_____
_____
_____
_____
_____
_____
_____
_____
_____
_____
_____
_____
_____
_____
_____
_____

24 Sunday

25 Monday

26 Tuesday

27 Wednesday

28 Thursday

29 Friday

30 Saturday

Notes

top priorities for this week

_____

_____

_____

_____

_____

Victories for the week

looking ahead to next week

_____

_____

_____

_____

_____

_____

_____

May 31-June 6

This Week

_____
_____
_____
_____
_____
_____
_____
_____
_____
_____
_____
_____
_____
_____
_____
_____
_____
_____
_____

31 Sunday	
1 Monday	
2 Tuesday	
3 Wednesday	

4   Thursday

5   Friday

6   Saturday

Notes

top priorities for this week

Victories for the week

looking ahead to next week

June 7-13

This Week

_____
_____
_____
_____
_____
_____
_____
_____
_____
_____
_____
_____
_____
_____
_____
_____
_____
_____

7 Sunday

8 Monday

9 Tuesday

10 Wednesday

11 Thursday

12 Friday

13 Saturday

Notes

Victories for the week

looking ahead to next week

June 14-20

This Week

_____
_____
_____
_____
_____
_____
_____
_____
_____
_____
_____
_____
_____
_____
_____
_____
_____
_____
_____
_____

14 Sunday
15 Monday
16 Tuesday
17 Wednesday

18   Thursday

19   Friday

20   Saturday

Notes

top priorities for this week

_____

_____

_____

_____

_____

_____

Victories for the week

looking ahead to next week

_____

_____

_____

_____

_____

_____

_____

_____

June 21-27

This Week

21 Sunday

22 Monday

23 Tuesday

24 Wednesday

25 Thursday

26 Friday

27 Saturday

Notes

top priorities for this week

_____
_____
_____
_____
_____
_____

Victories for the week

looking ahead to next week

_____
_____
_____
_____
_____
_____
_____
_____

June 28-July 4

This Week

_____
_____
_____
_____
_____
_____
_____
_____
_____
_____
_____
_____
_____
_____
_____
_____
_____
_____
_____
_____

28 Sunday
29 Monday
30 Tuesday
1 Wednesday

2 Thursday

3 Friday

4 Saturday

Notes

top priorities for this week

Victories for the week

looking ahead to next week

July 5-11

This Week

_____
_____
_____
_____
_____
_____
_____
_____
_____
_____
_____
_____
_____
_____
_____
_____
_____
_____
_____
_____
_____
_____

5 Sunday
6 Monday
7 Tuesday
8 Wednesday

9 Thursday

10 Friday

11 Saturday

Notes

top priorities for this week

_____
_____
_____
_____
_____

Victories for the week

looking ahead to next week

_____
_____
_____
_____
_____
_____
_____

July 12-18

This Week

_____
_____
_____
_____
_____
_____
_____
_____
_____
_____
_____
_____
_____
_____
_____
_____
_____
_____
_____
_____
_____

| 12 Sunday |
| 13 Monday |
| 14 Tuesday |
| 15 Wednesday |

16   Thursday

17   Friday

18   Saturday

Notes

top priorities for this week

_____
_____
_____
_____
_____

Victories for the week

looking ahead to next week

_____
_____
_____
_____
_____
_____
_____

July 19-25

This Week

_____
_____
_____
_____
_____
_____
_____
_____
_____
_____
_____
_____
_____
_____
_____
_____
_____
_____

19 Sunday

20 Monday

21 Tuesday

22 Wednesday

23 Thursday

24 Friday

25 Saturday

Notes

top priorities for this week

_____
_____
_____
_____
_____

Victories for the week

looking ahead to next week

_____
_____
_____
_____
_____
_____
_____

July 26-August 1

This Week

_____
_____
_____
_____
_____
_____
_____
_____
_____
_____
_____
_____
_____
_____
_____
_____
_____
_____
_____

26 Sunday
27 Monday
28 Tuesday
29 Wednesday

30 Thursday

31 Friday

1 Saturday

Notes

top priorities for this week

_____
_____
_____
_____
_____

Victories for the week

looking ahead to next week

_____
_____
_____
_____
_____
_____
_____
_____

August 2-8

This Week

_____
_____
_____
_____
_____
_____
_____
_____
_____
_____
_____
_____
_____
_____
_____
_____
_____
_____
_____

2 Sunday

3 Monday

4 Tuesday

5 Wednesday

6 Thursday

7 Friday

8 Saturday

Notes

top priorities for this week

_____
_____
_____
_____
_____
_____

Victories for the week

looking ahead to next week

_____
_____
_____
_____
_____
_____
_____
_____

August 9-15

This Week

_____
_____
_____
_____
_____
_____
_____
_____
_____
_____
_____
_____
_____
_____
_____
_____
_____
_____
_____
_____

9 Sunday

10 Monday

11 Tuesday

12 Wednesday

13 Thursday

14 Friday

15 Saturday

Notes

top priorities for this week
_____
_____
_____
_____
_____

Victories for the week

---

looking ahead to next week
_____
_____
_____
_____
_____
_____
_____
_____

August 16-22

This Week

_____
_____
_____
_____
_____
_____
_____
_____
_____
_____
_____
_____
_____
_____
_____
_____
_____
_____

16 Sunday

17 Monday

18 Tuesday

19 Wednesday

20 Thursday

21 Friday

22 Saturday

Notes

top priorities for this week

_____

_____

_____

_____

_____

Victories for the week

looking ahead to next week

_____

_____

_____

_____

_____

_____

_____

August 23-29

This Week

_____
_____
_____
_____
_____
_____
_____
_____
_____
_____
_____
_____
_____
_____
_____
_____
_____
_____
_____

23 Sunday
24 Monday
25 Tuesday
26 Wednesday

27 Thursday

28 Friday

29 Saturday

Notes

top priorities for this week

_____
_____
_____
_____
_____

Victories for the week

looking ahead to next week

_____
_____
_____
_____
_____
_____
_____

August 30-September 5

This Week

_____
_____
_____
_____
_____
_____
_____
_____
_____
_____
_____
_____
_____
_____
_____
_____
_____
_____
_____
_____
_____

30 Sunday

31 Monday

1 Tuesday

2 Wednesday

3 Thursday

4 Friday

5 Saturday

Notes

top priorities for this week

_____

_____

_____

_____

_____

Victories for the week

looking ahead to next week

_____

_____

_____

_____

_____

_____

_____

_____

September 6-12

This Week

_____
_____
_____
_____
_____
_____
_____
_____
_____
_____
_____
_____
_____
_____
_____
_____
_____
_____
_____
_____
_____

6 Sunday

7 Monday

8 Tuesday

9 Wednesday

10 Thursday

11 Friday

12 Saturday

Notes

top priorities for this week

_____

_____

_____

_____

_____

Victories for the week

looking ahead to next week

_____

_____

_____

_____

_____

_____

_____

_____

September 13-19

This Week

13 Sunday

14 Monday

15 Tuesday

16 Wednesday

17 Thursday

18 Friday

19 Saturday

Notes

top priorities for this week

_____
_____
_____
_____
_____

Victories for the week

looking ahead to next week

_____
_____
_____
_____
_____
_____
_____

September 20-26

This Week

_____
_____
_____
_____
_____
_____
_____
_____
_____
_____
_____
_____
_____
_____
_____
_____
_____
_____
_____
_____

20 Sunday
21 Monday
22 Tuesday
23 Wednesday

24 Thursday

25 Friday

26 Saturday

Notes

top priorities for this week

_____

_____

_____

_____

_____

Victories for the week

looking ahead to next week

_____

_____

_____

_____

_____

_____

_____

_____

September 27-October 3

This Week

_____
_____
_____
_____
_____
_____
_____
_____
_____
_____
_____
_____
_____
_____
_____
_____
_____
_____
_____

27 Sunday

28 Monday

29 Tuesday

27 Sunday

30 Wednesday

28 Tuesday

1 Thursday

2 Friday

3 Saturday

Notes

top priorities for this week

_____
_____
_____
_____
_____
_____

Victories for the week

looking ahead to next week

_____
_____
_____
_____
_____
_____
_____

October 4-10

This Week

_____

_____

_____

_____

_____

_____

_____

_____

_____

_____

_____

_____

_____

_____

_____

_____

_____

_____

_____

_____

4 Sunday
5 Monday
6 Tuesday
7 Wednesday

8 Thursday

9 Friday

10 Saturday

Notes

top priorities for this week

_____
_____
_____
_____
_____

Victories for the week

looking ahead to next week

_____
_____
_____
_____
_____
_____
_____

October 11-17

This Week

11 Sunday

12 Monday

13 Tuesday

14 Wednesday

15 Thursday

16 Friday

17 Saturday

Notes

top priorities for this week

_____
_____
_____
_____
_____

Victories for the week

looking ahead to next week

_____
_____
_____
_____
_____
_____
_____
_____

October 18-24

This Week

_____
_____
_____
_____
_____
_____
_____
_____
_____
_____
_____
_____
_____
_____
_____
_____
_____
_____

18 Sunday	
19 Monday	
20 Tuesday	
21 Wednesday	

22 Thursday

23 Friday

24 Saturday

Notes

_____

_____

_____

_____

_____

Victories for the week

looking ahead to next week

_____

_____

_____

_____

_____

_____

_____

October 25-31

This Week

_____

_____

_____

_____

_____

_____

_____

_____

_____

_____

_____

_____

_____

_____

_____

_____

_____

_____

_____

_____

25 Sunday

26 Monday

27 Tuesday

28 Wednesday

29 Thursday

30 Friday

31 Saturday

Notes

top priorities for this week

_____
_____
_____
_____
_____

Victories for the week

looking ahead to next week

_____
_____
_____
_____
_____
_____
_____

November 1-7

This Week

_____

_____

_____

_____

_____

_____

_____

_____

_____

_____

_____

_____

_____

_____

_____

_____

_____

_____

1 Sunday

2 Monday

3 Tuesday

4 Wednesday

5 Thursday

6 Friday

7 Saturday

Notes

Victories for the week

looking ahead to next week

November 8-14

This Week

_____
_____
_____
_____
_____
_____
_____
_____
_____
_____
_____
_____
_____
_____
_____
_____
_____
_____
_____
_____

8 Sunday

9 Monday

10 Tuesday

11 Wednesday

12 Thursday

13 Friday

14 Saturday

Notes

top priorities for this week

_____
_____
_____
_____
_____

Victories for the week

looking ahead to next week

_____
_____
_____
_____
_____
_____
_____

November 15-21

This Week

_____

_____

_____

_____

_____

_____

_____

_____

_____

_____

_____

_____

_____

_____

_____

_____

_____

_____

_____

_____

15 Sunday

16 Monday

17 Tuesday

18 Wednesday

19 Thursday

20 Friday

21 Saturday

Notes

top priorities for this week

_____
_____
_____
_____
_____

Victories for the week

looking ahead to next week

_____
_____
_____
_____
_____
_____
_____
_____

November 22-28

This Week

_____

_____

_____

_____

_____

_____

_____

_____

_____

_____

_____

_____

_____

_____

_____

_____

_____

_____

_____

_____

22 Sunday
23 Monday
24 Tuesday
25 Wednesday

26 Thursday

27 Friday

28 Saturday

Notes

top priorities for this week

_____
_____
_____
_____
_____

Victories for the week

looking ahead to next week

_____
_____
_____
_____
_____
_____
_____

November 29-December 5

This Week

_____
_____
_____
_____
_____
_____
_____
_____
_____
_____
_____
_____
_____
_____
_____
_____
_____
_____
_____
_____
_____

29 Sunday

30 Monday

1 Tuesday

2 Wednesday

3 Thursday

4 Friday

5 Saturday

Notes

top priorities for this week

_____
_____
_____
_____
_____

```
Victories for the week




```

looking ahead to next week

_____
_____
_____
_____
_____
_____
_____

December 6-12

This Week

_____
_____
_____
_____
_____
_____
_____
_____
_____
_____
_____
_____
_____
_____
_____
_____
_____
_____
_____
_____
_____

6 Sunday

7 Monday

8 Tuesday

9 Wednesday

10 Thursday

11 Friday

12 Saturday

Notes

top priorities for this week

_____
_____
_____
_____

Victories for the week

looking ahead to next week

_____
_____
_____
_____
_____
_____
_____

December 13-19

This Week

13 Sunday

14 Monday

15 Tuesday

16 Wednesday

17 Thursday

18 Friday

19 Saturday

Notes

top priorities for this week

_____
_____
_____
_____
_____

Victories for the week

looking ahead to next week

_____
_____
_____
_____
_____
_____
_____

December 20-26

This Week

_____
_____
_____
_____
_____
_____
_____
_____
_____
_____
_____
_____
_____
_____
_____
_____
_____
_____
_____

20 Sunday

21 Monday

22 Tuesday

23 Wednesday

24 Thursday

25 Friday

26 Saturday

Notes

top priorities for this week

_____
_____
_____
_____
_____

Victories for the week

looking ahead to next week

_____
_____
_____
_____
_____
_____
_____

December 27-January 2

This Week

_____
_____
_____
_____
_____
_____
_____
_____
_____
_____
_____
_____
_____
_____
_____
_____
_____
_____
_____
_____

27 Sunday

28 Monday

29 Tuesday

27 Sunday

30 Wednesday

31 Thursday

1 Friday

2 Saturday

Notes

top priorities for this week

_____

_____

_____

_____

_____

Victories for the week

looking ahead to next week

_____

_____

_____

_____

_____

_____

_____

Notes

Notes

Notes

Notes

Notes

Notes

Notes

Notes

Notes

Notes

Notes

Notes

Notes